Dear Jenne,

Wishes for much—
pleasure in your gardens

Much love,
Aunt Carolyn—
(Christmas 1992)

WITH ILLUSTRATIONS FROM THE COLLECTION OF THE
MUSEUM OF FINE ARTS, BOSTON

HUGH LAUTER LEVIN ASSOCIATES, INC., NEW YORK

DISTRIBUTED BY
MACMILLAN PUBLISHING COMPANY

ILLUSTRATIONS

Niels Emil Severin Holm
VIEW OF THE STRAITS OF MESSINA FROM A
COUNTRY HOUSE
1859
oil on canvas
32½ × 51½"
Tompkins Collection; Gift of John Goelet

John Singer Sargent
VILLA DI MARLIA: A FOUNTAIN
1910
watercolor
16 × 20¾"
Hayden Collection. Charles Henry Hayden Fund

Sir Lawrence Alma-Tadema
WOMAN AND FLOWERS
1868
oil on panel
19⅝ × 14⅝"
Gift of Edward Jackson Holmes

Emil Nolde
IRIS
20th-century
watercolor
18½ × 13½"
Seth K. Sweetser Fund

John Sloan
FLOWERS IN SPRING
c. 1920
oil on canvas
30 × 25"
Gift of Amelia E. White

Ross Sterling Turner
A GARDEN IS A SEA OF FLOWERS
1912
watercolor
20½ × 30½"
Gift of the estate of Nellie P. Carter

Jean François Millet
POTATO PLANTERS
19th-century
oil on canvas
32½ × 39⅞"
Gift of Quincy Adams Shaw through Quincy A. Shaw, Jr.
and Mrs. Marian Shaw Haughton

Mary Stevenson Cassatt
GATHERING FRUIT
c. 1893
drypoint and aquatint in color
16¼ × 11¾"
Gift of William Emerson and Charles Henry Hayden Fund

Gustave Caillebotte
FRUIT DISPLAYED ON A STAND
19th-century
oil on canvas
30⅛ × 39⅝"
Fanny P. Mason Fund in Memory of Alice Thevin

Chao Shu-ju
SUMMER BLOSSOMS
1926
ink and color on paper
44¾ × 19⅝"
Keith McLeod Fund

John La Farge
APPLE BLOSSOMS
19th-century
watercolor
10⅙ × 7⅝"
Bequest of Mrs. Henry Lee Higginson

Claude Monet
WATER LILIES (I)
1905
oil on canvas
35¼ × 39½"
Gift of Edward Jackson Holmes

Anonymous
WILSON'S ALBANY (STRAWBERRIES) from
D.M. Dewey's NURSERYMAN'S POCKET BOOK OF
SPECIMEN FRUIT AND FLOWERS
1875
stencil and watercolor
8¾ × 5¼"
Gift of Mrs. Alan Tawse

Joseph Stella
CACTUS AND TROPICAL FOLIAGE
c. 1922
watercolor over graphite
18⅛ × 24⅛"
Sophie M. Friedman Fund

French or Franco-Flemish
NARCISSUS from Ovid's *METAMORPHOSES*
late 15th- or early 16th-century
tapestry; wool and silk
111 × 122½"
Charles Potter Kling Fund

Calligraphy by Jeanne Greco

© 1986 by Hugh Lauter Levin Associates, Inc.
All rights reserved.

Printed in Japan

ISBN 0-88363-187-3

Contents

Through gardening we are given
the key to some of Nature's most
inspiring secrets; and as we work
together with the elements to
raise flowers, fruits, and vegetables,
we are permitted to catch many a
glimpse of Nature's miracles and
we are given many of her gifts.

In these pages you can record the
pleasures of your gardening year.
This book will store these facts,
and in these notes your garden will
be in bloom at all seasons and for
all time.

My Garden

*No occupation is as delightful to me
as the culture of the earth, and no
culture comparable to that of the garden*

Thomas Jefferson

This is the garden of

____

____

____

Its location is

____

____

____

It specializes in

____

____

____

____

VIEW OF THE STRAITS OF MESSINA FROM A COUNTRY HOUSE—Niels Emil Severin Holm

There is a garden…
Where roses and white lilies grow;
A heavenly paradise is that place.

Thomas Campion

History

Date started ______________________________

Size ______________________________

Type of soil ______________________________

Climate and / or zone ______________________________

Light ______________________________

Past Plantings of Note

Perennials ______________________________

____

Shrubs and trees ______________________________

____

Bulbs ______________________________

____

Annuals ______________________________

____

VILLA DI MARLIA: A FOUNTAIN—John Singer Sargent

*Men plant flowers because it represents
a way of affirming the renewability of life—
watching them grow each year, you know
you can do it again next year.*   *Anonymous*

Future Plantings and Projects
Hopes and Goals

The Garden Plan
Draw the layout of your garden here

Of all the flowers in the field,
Then I love most this flower red and white,
Such as men call daisies . . .

Geoffrey Chaucer

My Favorite Flowers

Perennials and Biennials _______________

____

____

Bulbs _________________________________

____

Flowering shrubs and trees _____________

Annuals _______________________________

My favorite garden colors ______________

____

____

WOMAN AND FLOWERS—*Sir Lawrence Alma-Tadema*

Not every soil can bear all things.

Virgil

Soil Preparation

When started _______________________________

____

____

____

Condition of soil _______________________________

____

Type of soil _______________________________

pH factor _______________________________

Soil conditioners used _______________________________

____

Long before [man] existed the land was in fact regularly plowed, and still continues to be thus plowed, by earthworms.   Charles Darwin

Fertilizers

Types

____

____

____

____

____

Where applied

____

____

____

____

____

Dates applied

____

____

____

____

____

____

____

____

God Almighty first planted a garden

Sir Francis Bacon

Seeds Ordered or Purchased

Type of seed	Ordered from

Comments

IRIS—Emil Nolde

*Short of Aphrodite, there is nothing
lovelier on this planet than a flower.*

Peter Tompkins

Flowers Planted—Annuals

Started indoors   Date

____

____

Planted outdoors   Location

____

____

Purchased in flats   Source

____

____

Biennials

How started   Date started   Source

____

____

"Let us plant now and be merry, for next autumn we may be ruined." After all, if I spend £20 on plants now, they will go on increasing in beauty for years.

Victoria Sackville-West

Perennials

Types	Date planted & position	Source
From division		
From cuttings		
From seeds		

Comments

If I had but two loaves of bread, I would
sell one and buy hyacinths, for they would
feed my soul.   *The Koran*

Bulbs Planted

Type	Where planted	Source

Comments

FLOWERS IN SPRING—John Sloan

A man of words and not of deeds,
Is like a garden full of weeds.

Mother Goose

Weeding Schedule

*Sweet April showers
Do spring May flowers.*

Thomas Tusser

Watering Schedule

My Flower Garden

How does the meadow flower its bloom unfold?
Because the lovely little flower is free
Down to its roots, and, in that freedom, bold.

William Wordsworth

Record of Bloom

Flower	Date

A GARDEN IS A SEA OF FLOWERS—Ross Sterling Turner

My Flower Garden

Shed no tear! O shed no tear!
The flower will bloom another year!
Weep no more! Weep no more!
Young buds sleep in the root's white core.

John Keats

Storage of Bulbs, Corms and Tender Plants

Type	How & where stored

Everything that grows,
Holds in perfection but a little moment.

William Shakespeare

Miscellaneous Notes

The earth bringeth forth fruit of herself;
first the blade, then the ear; after that
the full corn in the ear.   *Mark 4:28*

Soil Preparation

POTATO PLANTERS—*Jean François Millet*

To own a bit of ground, to scratch it with a hoe,
to plant seeds, and watch the renewal of life—
this is the commonest delight of the race,
the most satisfactory thing a man can do.

Charles Dudley Warner

Seed Sowing

Started indoors	Date	Source

Sown in the garden

Comments

Draw the layout here

*All the fruits will outdo what the
flowers have started.*

François de Malherbe

Transplanting, pruning, staking, etc.

Comments

GATHERING FRUIT—Mary Stevenson Cassatt

Long about knee deep in June,
'Bout the time Strawberries melts
On the vine.

James Whitcomb Riley

Fertilizing Schedule

Who loves a garden still his Eden keeps,
Perennial pleasures, plants, and wholesome
harvest reaps.
Amos Bronson Alcott

Mulching, Weeding and Watering Schedule

*Training is everything. The peach was once a
bitter almond; cauliflower is nothing but a
cabbage with a college education.*

Mark Twain

The Harvest

Date	What	Quantity	Comments

FRUIT DISPLAYED ON A STAND—Gustave Caillebotte

My Vegetable, Fruit & Herb Garden

Much pleasure we have lost, while we abstained
From the delightful fruit, nor known til now,
True relish, tasting.

John Milton

Canning, Preserving, Freezing and Drying

Date	What	Quantity	Comments

The first cuckoo of the year provokes a silent prayer, as also the first asparagus and the first green pea.

Harold Nicolson

Miscellaneous Notes

My Trees, Shrubs & Lawn

Holy Mother Earth, the trees and all nature
are witnesses of your thoughts and deeds.

Winnebago Indian Saying

Extant Plantings and Future Plans

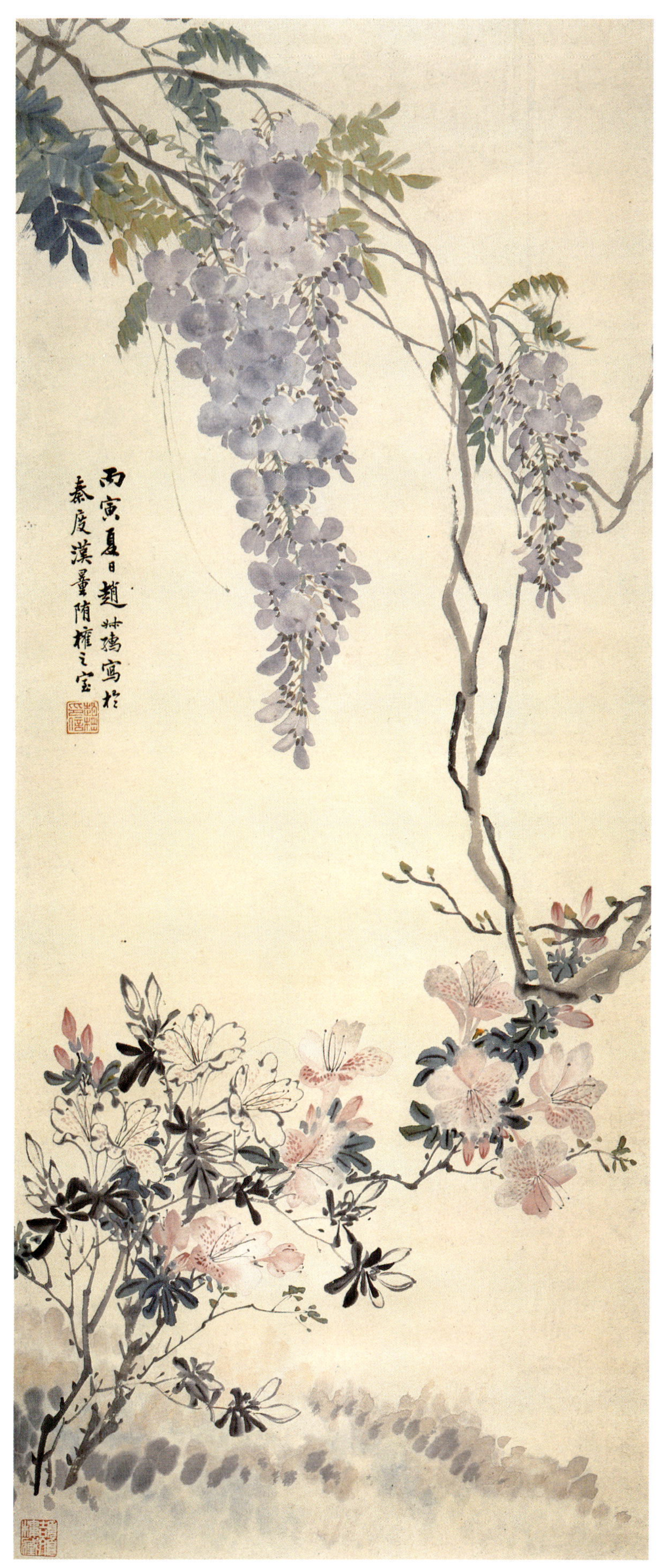

SUMMER BLOSSOMS—*Chao Shu-ju*

*Like snow, dandelions enchant children
but dismay adults.*   Barbara Pond

Fertilizing   Date

Weed control

Mowing schedule

*I believe a leaf of grass is no less
than the journey-work of the stars.*

Walt Whitman

New Plantings

Types	Location

Comments

Myriads of rivulets running through the lawn,
The moan of doves in the immemorial elms
And murmuring of innumerable bees.

Alfred Lord Tennyson

Pruning, Fertilizing and Watering Schedule

Task	Date

APPLE BLOSSOMS—John La Farge

Weather

O farmers, pray that your summers
be wet and your winters clear.
Virgil

First frost

Last frost

____

____

____

Heat spells

____

____

____

Rainfall and dry spells

____

____

____

____

Weather

Now the summer came to pass,
And the flowers through the grass
Joyously sprang,
While all the tribes of birds sang.

Walther von der Vogelweide

Miscellaneous Notes and Comments

We must cultivate our garden

Voltaire

Date	Item	Cost	Comments

WATER LILIES (I)—Claude Monet

Joy… entices flowers from seeds,
Suns from the firmament.

Friedrich von Schiller

Additional Garden Plan

Draw your plan here

Spring, the sweet spring, is the year's
   pleasant king;
Then blooms each thing...
Cold doth not sting, the pretty birds do sing...

Thomas Nashe

WILSON'S ALBANY (STRAWBERRIES)—Anonymous

I know a bank whereon the wild thyme blows,
Where oxlips and the nodding violet grows
Quite overcanopied with luscious woodbine,
With sweet musk-roses and with eglantine.

William Shakespeare

Garden _______________________________________

Location _____________________________________

Date visited _________________________________

Plantings of interest & good ideas ___________

____

Comments _____________________________________

____

Garden _______________________________________

Location _____________________________________

Date visited _________________________________

Plantings of interest & good ideas ___________

____

Comments _____________________________________

____

*Consider the lilies of the field, how they grow;
they toil not, neither do they spin… even
Solomon in all his glory was not arrayed like
one of these.*

Matthew 6:28-29

Garden ___________________________

Location ___________________________

Date visited ___________________________

Plantings of interest & good ideas ___________

____

Comments ___________________________

____

Garden ___________________________

Location ___________________________

Date visited ___________________________

Plantings of interest & good ideas ___________

____

Comments ___________________________

____

Rose is a rose is a rose is a rose.

Gertrude Stein

Additional Notes and Comments

CACTUS AND TROPICAL FOLIAGE—Joseph Stella

No one knows
Through what wild centuries
Roves back the rose.

Walter de la Mare

Unusual and Helpful Garden Lore
I Have Learned or Read

NARCISSUS—French or Franco-Flemish

Title ______________________________
Author ______________________________
Comments ______________________________
____

Title ______________________________
Author ______________________________
Comments ______________________________
____

Title ______________________________
Author ______________________________
Comments ______________________________
____

Title ______________________________
Author ______________________________
Comments ______________________________
____

Checklist of Supplies

Mulch

Peat moss

Potting soil

Sand

Vermiculite or Perlite

Leafmold or compost

Manure

Organic fertilizer

Inorganic fertilizer

Flats

Clay pots

Peat pots for seedlings

Labels

Waterproof marking pens

Chicken wire

Burlap

Plastic sheeting

Stakes

Twine

Twisters

Trash bags

Gloves

Cultivating rake

Leaf and/or grass rake

Hoe

Digging spade

Weeder/cultivator

Spading fork

Bulb planter

Trowel

Cutting shears

Grass shears

Hedge shears

Lawnmower

Power saw

Wheelbarrow

Garden cart

Watering can

Hose

Sprinkler attachments

5-gallon plastic pails

Miscellaneous:

Nurseries; Seed, Plant and Bulb Sources; Garden Centers and Garden Supply Sources; Garden Clubs and Organizations; Lawn Care; etc.